This book belongs to:

Cora was a pleasant little girl. She lived with her Mummy, Daddy and her big brother Tim. She loved doing things that were new and exciting. She was not a shy girl and was not easily frightened by things. You could say she was courageous and confident!

When she was a child, Cora wanted to be a vet. She loved animals and her Mummy encouraged her by bringing home abandoned animals she had rescued.

When she was not looking after the dogs, cats and birds that her Mummy had rescued, Cora loved going to ballet classes. She would put on her purple leotard, special tights and ballet shoes. Her stretches helped her warm up and do her spins and dance steps.

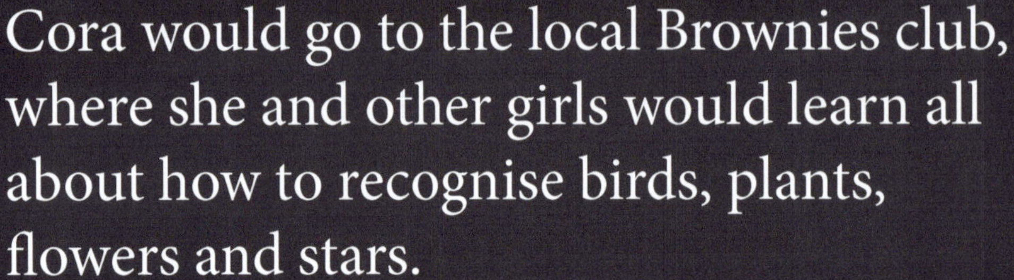

Cora would go to the local Brownies club, where she and other girls would learn all about how to recognise birds, plants, flowers and stars.

They would also go on camping trips – doing practical things like learning to tie knots and fishing.

She enjoyed sitting around the large camp-fire at night with her friends and their leaders. They would drink hot chocolate and sing songs heartily as the flames quivered and danced.

Cora's Daddy
was a lorry driver.
He worked shifts for
8 hours each day and
had to drive a long way
for work, taking important
items to lots of places around
Europe.

He often left their home at 2 o'clock
in the morning and drive to the depot
where his lorry was waiting. He would
climb into the cabin and turn on the
engine that growled as its big wheels moved
in synchrony.

Tim and Cora's Mummy worked as a meal assistant at their school. She was always home in the morning and made them a yummy breakfast to start the day.

She helped them with their school lunches and walked home with them in the afternoon.

Cora did not mind getting her hands dirty. When there was something important to do. She enjoyed helping her Daddy with light engineering tasks – such as fixing cars for the family and friends in the local town who would call them if their car was broken down.

YZ21OCQ

Cora's Daddy showed her what all of the different tools were in his garage and how they were used. Some of them were somewhat heavy and many were greasy. Her Daddy was very clever.

One of the cars they repaired was very old and various parts were missing. He managed to fix the car with bits and pieces and it worked!

Cora's big brother was very kind and caring towards her. He helped her learn to tie her shoelaces and listened to her reading if Mummy was too busy cooking dinner in the kitchen.

After supper, they would walk their dogs together along the local high street on the way to the park. Cora loved to see all the new small businesses popping up in the neighbourhood.

One Autumn, Cora and Tim wanted to raise money to pay for Christmas presents. They started a car wash business in the street where they lived. They would go from door to door with sponges and buckets. When neighbours opened their doors, Cora and Tim would smile and offer a good price for making their cars clean and shiny.

It was hard work to do a good job but the neighbours were very happy. They earned quite a lot of money and were able to buy gifts for their parents, cousins and friends.

Cora did well at school, she worked hard, was obedient to her teachers and was liked by the other pupils. When she was in senior school she succeeded in her school examinations.

She applied to university and got a place to study English Literature. She was the first person in her family to go to university and this made them very proud!

When her brother Tim grew older, he began to travel to other parts of the world in relation to his work. He travelled to Africa and became a micro-farmer in a country called Burundi.

This meant that he had some land that was not huge in size but enabled him and a team of local people to have a sense of purpose and grow fruit and vegetables for their families.

This project was very exciting for Cora as she was able to travel to see her brother there and made friends with lots of the people in the area. She would take small gifts of pencils, crayons, notebooks and toiletries in her suitcase. The children in the village near the farm would run to see her when she arrived with many large bags of goodies!

After three years of hard work, Cora graduated from University. She wondered what she should do next when the opportunity for her to work as a personal assistant in a bank arose! She did this with the plan to find a different job that was linked to her English literature degree later on.

Cora was very industrious, she worked at the bank during the day and worked in a restaurant in the evenings and at weekends. She found the job in the bank quite interesting because she realised that banking is about helping people and this was something she had always wanted to do.

Cora worked in the Financial Services section of the bank and did a range of junior roles to help small businesses like restaurants, florists, cafés and to get started.

The people she worked with were very nice and they taught her so many aspects of banking and finance. She got better and better at the different tasks and projects.

Petals & Posies
THE Cosy Café
OPEN

Cora now has lots of experience and works for a big bank. She works with companies around the world. She has a big team of 85 people working with her and they do wonderful things for lots of people. Some of the people she manages live very far away in Hong Kong and Vietnam.

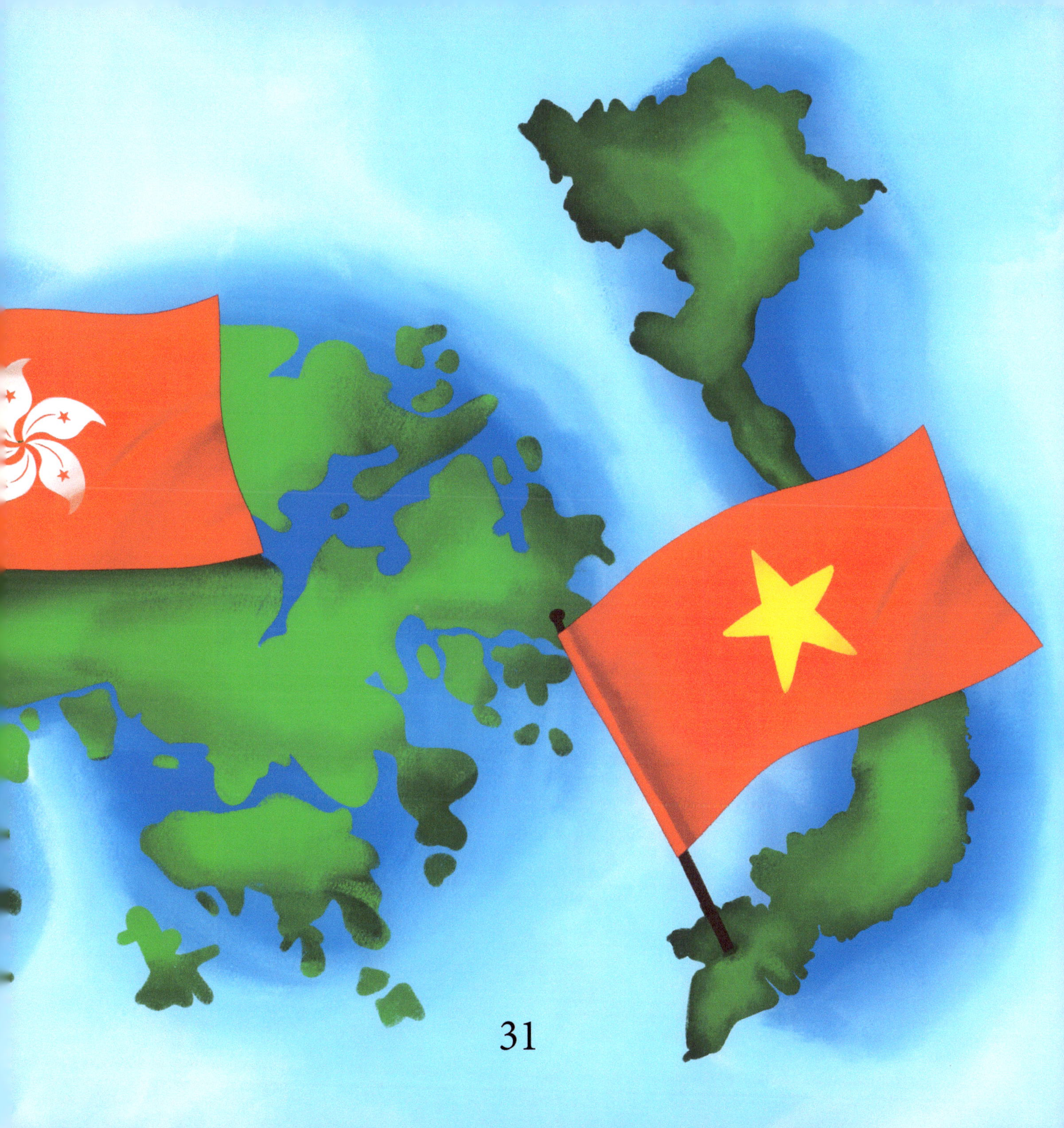

As Cora works with people in other countries, she is now able to speak French, German and Cantonese.

In her spare time, Cora rescues dogs. The dogs make Cora feel happy and they can be playful. Being an investment banker and helping businesses to start and flourish is something that Cora does well.

BANK

Cora is very passionate about her job where she meets so many entrepreneurs and small business owners who come to her for help. She enjoys teaching them about money and giving them financial advice.

You can be an impressive investment banker, just like Cora!

BANK

If you want to be an impressive investment banker or, take a look at these references to learn how!

For Kids:

NatWest
Practise spotting value for money as you trade with three outlandish alien shopkeepers for a range of space commodities.
https://natwest.mymoneysense.com/students/students-8-12/space-trader/

Cool Kid Facts
Information page for kids on the history of banking and how banks work.
https://www.coolkidfacts.com/how-banks-work/

Ducksters
Information page for kids on economics.
https://www.ducksters.com/money/economics.php

For parents and guardians:

The Complete University Guide
Comprehensive UK university league tables for accounting and finance.
https://www.thecompleteuniversityguide.co.uk/league-tables/rankings/accounting-and-finance

Target Careers
Information on how to begin a career in finance.
https://targetcareers.co.uk/career-sectors/finance/70-how-do-i-get-into-finance

Indeed.com
Advice page on career paths within banking.
https://www.indeed.com/career-advice/career-development/career-paths-banking

What do you want to be when you grow up? Draw it below!

Notes!

....

....

....

....

....

....

....

....

....

....

....

....

....

....

Check out some other books in the series!

www.ingramcontent.com/pod-product-compliance
Lightning Source LLC
LaVergne TN
LVHW071207160826
845679LV00003B/770

* 9 7 8 1 9 1 7 1 6 2 1 7 3 *